Ex Libris

# Christmas Memories

The holidays are a warm and festive time of year when family and friends come together to celebrate the season and create lifelong memories. Our *Christmas Memories* gift book is designed for you to record all the treasured moments of this special time of year. Plan your holiday schedules from year to year with our calendar grids and record the gifts you give as well as those you receive in a special section of the journal. This gift book will be a keepsake to share with family and friends for years to come.

$\mathcal{A}$ little season

of love and laughter,

of light and life

~A. L. Gordon

# December

| Sun. | Mon. | Tues. | Wed. |
|------|------|-------|------|
|      |      |       |      |
|      |      |       |      |
|      |      |       |      |
|      |      |       |      |
|      |      |       |      |

*year* _____

| Thurs. | Fri. | Sat. |
|---|---|---|
|  |  |  |
|  |  |  |
|  |  |  |
|  |  |  |
|  |  |  |

# December

| Sun. | Mon. | Tues. | Wed. |
|------|------|-------|------|
|      |      |       |      |
|      |      |       |      |
|      |      |       |      |
|      |      |       |      |
|      |      |       |      |

*year*____

| Thurs. | Fri. | Sat. |
|---|---|---|
| | | |
| | | |
| | | |
| | | |
| | | |

# December

| Sun. | Mon. | Tues. | Wed. |
|------|------|-------|------|
|      |      |       |      |
|      |      |       |      |
|      |      |       |      |
|      |      |       |      |
|      |      |       |      |

*year*_____

| Thurs. | Fri. | Sat. |
|--------|------|------|
|        |      |      |
|        |      |      |
|        |      |      |
|        |      |      |
|        |      |      |

# December

| Sun. | Mon. | Tues. | Wed. |
|------|------|-------|------|
|      |      |       |      |
|      |      |       |      |
|      |      |       |      |
|      |      |       |      |
|      |      |       |      |

*year*＿＿＿＿

| Thurs. | Fri. | Sat. |
|--------|------|------|
|        |      |      |
|        |      |      |
|        |      |      |
|        |      |      |
|        |      |      |

# December

| Sun. | Mon. | Tues. | Wed. |
|------|------|-------|------|
|      |      |       |      |
|      |      |       |      |
|      |      |       |      |
|      |      |       |      |
|      |      |       |      |

*year*_____

| Thurs. | Fri. | Sat. |
|---|---|---|
| | | |
| | | |
| | | |
| | | |
| | | |

# December

| Sun. | Mon. | Tues. | Wed. |
|------|------|-------|------|
|      |      |       |      |
|      |      |       |      |
|      |      |       |      |
|      |      |       |      |
|      |      |       |      |

*year* _____

| Thurs. | Fri. | Sat. |
|--------|------|------|
|        |      |      |
|        |      |      |
|        |      |      |
|        |      |      |
|        |      |      |

# December

| Sun. | Mon. | Tues. | Wed. |
|------|------|-------|------|
|      |      |       |      |
|      |      |       |      |
|      |      |       |      |
|      |      |       |      |
|      |      |       |      |

*year*_____

| Thurs. | Fri. | Sat. |
|--------|------|------|
|        |      |      |
|        |      |      |
|        |      |      |
|        |      |      |
|        |      |      |

# December

| Sun. | Mon. | Tues. | Wed. |
|------|------|-------|------|
|      |      |       |      |
|      |      |       |      |
|      |      |       |      |
|      |      |       |      |
|      |      |       |      |

_year_ _____

| Thurs. | Fri. | Sat. |
|--------|------|------|
| | | |
| | | |
| | | |
| | | |
| | | |

# December

| Sun. | Mon. | Tues. | Wed. |
|------|------|-------|------|
|      |      |       |      |
|      |      |       |      |
|      |      |       |      |
|      |      |       |      |
|      |      |       |      |

*year*_____

| Thurs. | Fri. | Sat. |
|---|---|---|
| | | |
| | | |
| | | |
| | | |
| | | |

# December

| Sun. | Mon. | Tues. | Wed. |
|------|------|-------|------|
|      |      |       |      |
|      |      |       |      |
|      |      |       |      |
|      |      |       |      |
|      |      |       |      |

*year* _____

| Thurs. | Fri. | Sat. |
|--------|------|------|
|        |      |      |
|        |      |      |
|        |      |      |
|        |      |      |
|        |      |      |

$\mathcal{A}$ loving heart

is the truest wisdom

~ Charles Dickens

The heart of the giver

makes the gift

dear and precious.

~ Martin Luther

# Gifts Given

# Gifts Received

# Gifts Given

# Gifts Received

# Gifts Given

# Gifts Received

_____

_____

_____

_____

_____

_____

_____

_____

_____

_____

_____

_____

_____

_____

_____

_____

_____

_____

_____

_____

_____

_____

_____

# Gifts Given

# Gifts Received

_____

_____

_____

_____

_____

_____

_____

_____

_____

_____

_____

_____

_____

_____

_____

_____

_____

_____

_____

_____

_____

# Gifts Given

# Gifts Received

# Gifts Given

# Gifts Received

# Gifts Given

# Gifts Received

# Gifts Given

# Gifts Received

# Gifts Given

# Gifts Received

_____

_____

_____

_____

_____

_____

_____

_____

_____

_____

_____

_____

_____

_____

_____

_____

_____

_____

_____

_____

_____

# Gifts Given

# Gifts Received

# Gifts Given

# Gifts Received

_____

_____

_____

_____

_____

_____

_____

_____

_____

_____

_____

_____

_____

_____

_____

_____

_____

_____

_____

_____

_____

*Victoria* ™

From the pages of Victoria Magazine.
Victoria is a trademark of The Hearst Corporation.
Photograph by Toshi Otsuki.
Printed in Hong Kong exclusively for
MARCEL SCHURMAN COMPANY
A Division of Schurman Fine Papers
Fairfield, CA  No. 33063